# TURNER FIRST YEAR MCQ

## OBJECTIVE QUESTION ANSWERS

MANOJ DOLE

Digitization is the need of the time. In the future, training in industrial training institutes will need to be conducted using online internet to make training more convenient and easy. E-books containing a set of MCQ questions will be made available to the trainees as they need to be more accustomed to the multiple choice questions MCQ to prepare for the online exams taking place in their industrial training institutes.

With all these factors in mind, Mr. Manoj Madhukar Dole Instructor, Industrial Training Institute, Satara, has written books according to the new annual system and NSQF-5 syllabus. And they've created theoretical mobile apps and blogs to make training easier, and made all these educational materials available for download on the world famous websites Google Play Store, Amazon and Apple Book Store.

The books were published by Hon'ble Joint Director Shri Rajendra Ghume Saheb Regional Office of Vocational Education and Training, Pune on 9/1/2019, at this time Shri Prakash Saigavkar Saheb Principal Government Industrial Training Institute Aundh Pune, Shri Tukaram Misal Saheb Principal Govt. Q. Sanstha Satara, Shri Sachin Dhumal Saheb District Vocational Education and Training Officer Satara, Shri Yatin Pargaonkar Saheb Principal Govt. Q. Sanstha Kolhapur, Shri Vikas Teke Saheb Inspector Vocational Education and Training Regional Office Pune, Palekar Foods Products Pvt. Ltd. Entrepreneurial Chairman of Satara Mr. Nilkanthrao Palekar Saheb, Chairman of Hira Foods Mr. Ibrahim Baba Tamboli Saheb, Mrs. Shalmali Pawar Headmaster Government Technical School Center Satara and other dignitaries were present on the occasion.

# Contents

# Prologue

**Turner First Year MCQ** is a simple e-Book for ITI Engineering Course Turner, First Year, Sem- 1 & 2, Revised NSQ F-5 Syllabus in 2022, It contains objective questions with underlined & bold correct answers MCQ covering all topics including all about basic fitting & different turning including setting of different shaped job on different chucks. The different turning operations – Plain, Facing, Drilling, Boring (counter and stepped) Grooving, Parallel turning, Stepped turning, Parting, Chamfering, U-cut, Reaming, Internal recess & Knurling., grinding of different cutting tools viz., V tool, side cutting, parting and thread cutting (both LH & RH), axial slip of main spindle, true running of head stock, parallelism of main spindle and alignment of both the centre axial slip of main spindle, true running of head stock, parallelism of main spindle and alignment of both the centres, The safety aspects covers components like OSH&E, PPE, Fire extinguisher, First Aid and in addition 5S, different components (Form tool, Compound slide, Tail stock offset, taper turning attachment) & parameters (feed, speed, depth of cut) of lathe for taper/ angular turning of jobs, Different boring operations (plain, stepped and eccentric), Different thread cutting (BSW, Metric, Square, ACME, Buttress), different accessories of lathe (Driving Plate, Steady rest, dog carrier and different centres), preventive maintenance of lathe and grinding machine and lots more.

We add new question answers with each new version. Please email us in case of any errors/omissions. This is arguably the largest and best e-Book for All engineering multiple choice questions and answers.

As a student you can use it for your exam prep. This e-Book is also useful for professors to refresh material.

# Foreword

Vocational education and training is imparted through the Department of Vocational Education and Training through the Department of Business Education and Business Practical to supply multi-skilled artisans in line with the rapidly growing demand in the industrial sector in the 21$^{st}$ century. All the occupations within the institutions are important, as the trainees from these occupations develop multi-skills as per the demands of the industry.

with the noble intention of making available MCQ e-books suitable for all businesses, considering that all the examinations in all the industries in the industrial sector are conducted online and include MCQ method questions. Mr. Manoj Madhukar Dole has written a very good e-book on MCQ method as per the new annual syllabus. This e-book will definitely be a guide for all the trainees, trainee candidates, training instructors and others concerned.

The author of the book is Mr. Manoj Madhukar Dole, Instructor Gov. ITI Satara has 17 years of training experience. Written as a new annual pattern, this e-book incorporates modern digital QR Code technology to understand the layout, simple language, and simple syntax, diagrams and videos for each subject. So I am sure that this e-book will definitely be useful for in-depth study and exam practice. The work they have done is certainly commendable.

Mr. Tukaram Misal
Principal Government Industrial Training Institute Satara.

# Preface

DGET New Delhi and CSTARI Kolkata have been implementing an annual pattern for all businesses in ITI since the August 2018 session. The examination system will also be changed and it will be online from this year and since all the questions are of Objective Type (MCQ), the trainees are in dire need of in-depth study. It is with this in mind that we are delighted to present the books based on the old NIMI pattern and a complete overview of the new annual pattern, and we hope that these books will be a guide for all business directors and trainees. Is.

For writing these books, Johar Awate Saheb, Principal of ITI Akluj. Former Principal of ITI Satara Saigavkar Saheb, Assistant Director Shri Chandrakant Dhekne Saheb Regional Office of Vocational Education and Training, Pune, District Vocational Education and Training Officer Sachin Dhumal Saheb and Headmaster Government Technical School Kendra Shalmali Pawar Madam and son Adhiraj Dole, mother Kusum Dole, I am very grateful to my father Madhukar Dole and wife Ashwini Dole for their special guidance and cooperation from time to time.

Also, in a very short period of time, the book was reviewed by Shri Rajendra Ghume Saheb, Joint Director, Vocational Education and Training Regional Office, Pune, for his invaluable time in publishing the book. I am sincerely grateful for their feedback.

I am grateful to the Instructor of ITI Satara for there continuous support from the very beginning of writing the book.

From this book, I consider myself blessed to have shared my thoughts on e-learning with you. I will not claim that this book is perfect, because considering the perfection, this book is an attempt and is in its infancy. They will be valuable for improvement if they are tested and suggested.

Manoj Dole
Dated 9/1/2019

# Acknowledgements

The industrial training and theoretical examination system of our industrial training institutes and these changes have been accepted by the craft instructors and the trainees. Theoretical examinations conducted in your industrial training institutes are also conducted online. Since these examinations are of multiple choice MCQ method, the trainees will need to get more practice of such questions.

With all these considerations in mind, Mr. Manoj Madhukar, Director, Dole Crafts, Katari Industrial Training Institute, Satara, has done a thorough study and with his diligent work and added his keen intellect, according to the new annual system and NSQF-5 syllabus, e-book of Katari and other machine trades. -Book) and they have created mobile apps and blogs on theoretical topics to make training easier and have made all these educational materials available for download on the world famous websites Google Play Store, Amazon and Apple Book Store. Training has been made easier by creating a print version and using advanced techniques like QR Code.

All these educational materials will definitely be a guide for all the trainees for in-depth study and for the craft instructors and other concerned who are imparting vocational training.

# CHAPTER ONE

# Turner First Year MCQ Drawings

Online Test Exam

ITI Books

CNC Course

AutoCAD CAM

JOB & Apprentice

Online Theory

Computer Course

Trading Course

Web Designing

MSCIT Course

Shopping Business

Internet Business

Remotasks Course

Online Services

Top Sportsmans

Indian Army

Freedom Fighters

Top Scientists

Social Reformers

Motivational Speaker

Top Richest People

Join WhatsApp Group

Join Facebook Group

Like Facebook Page

PAN / Adhar / Licence
Passport

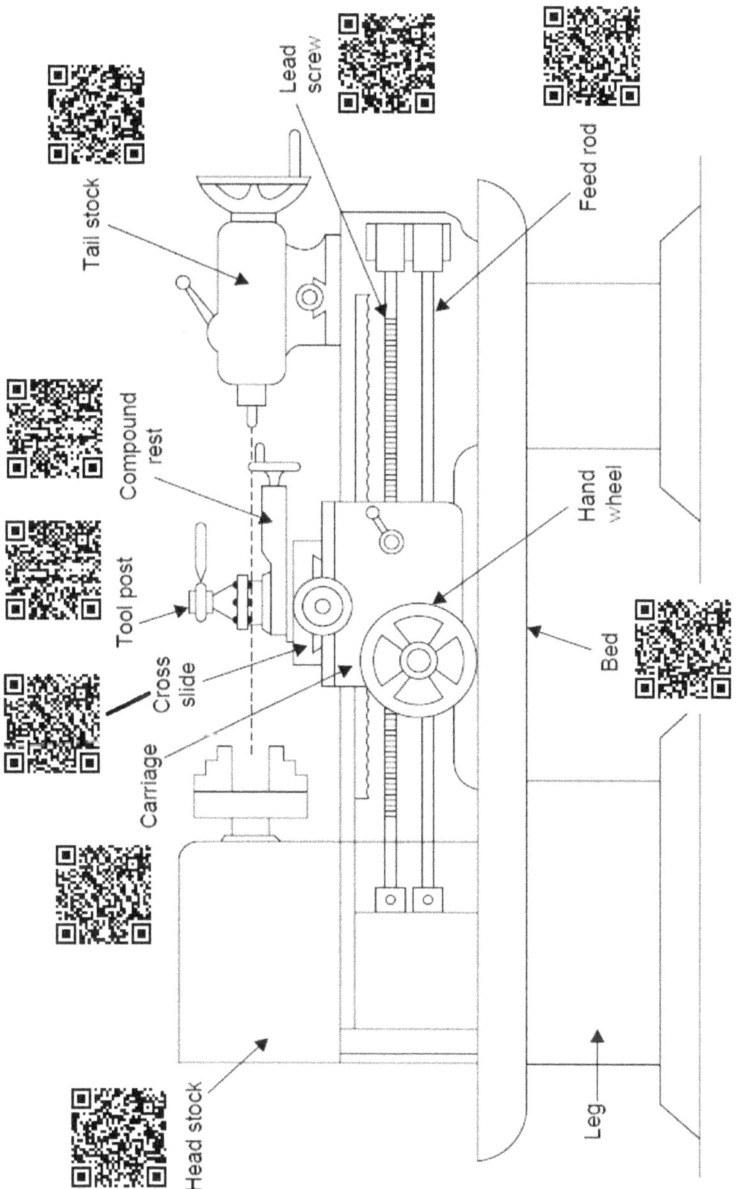


Lathe Machine

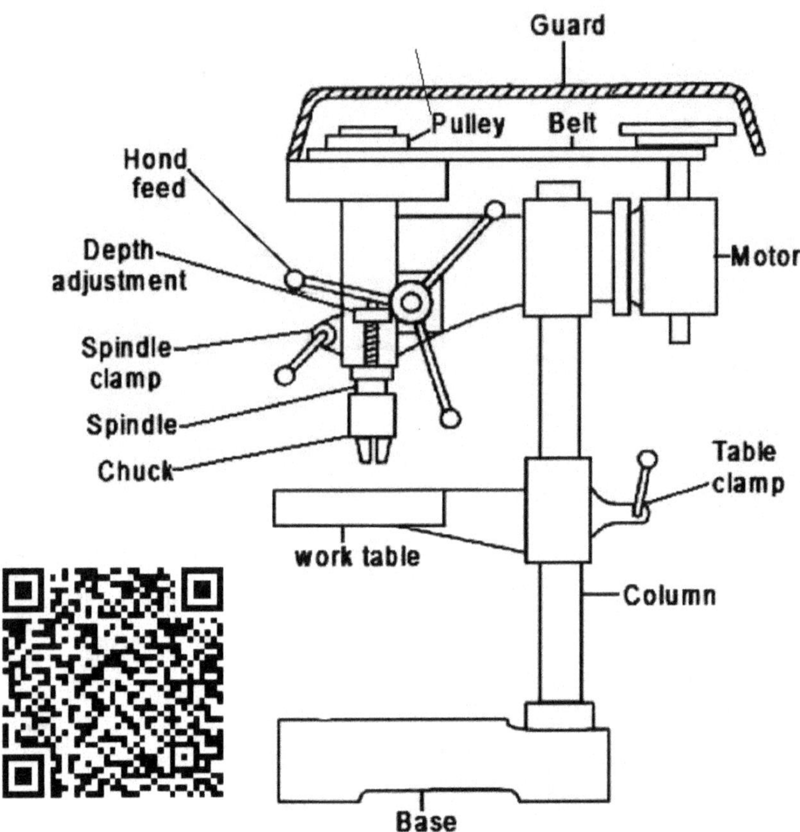


# Piller Drilling Machine

Drilling Machine

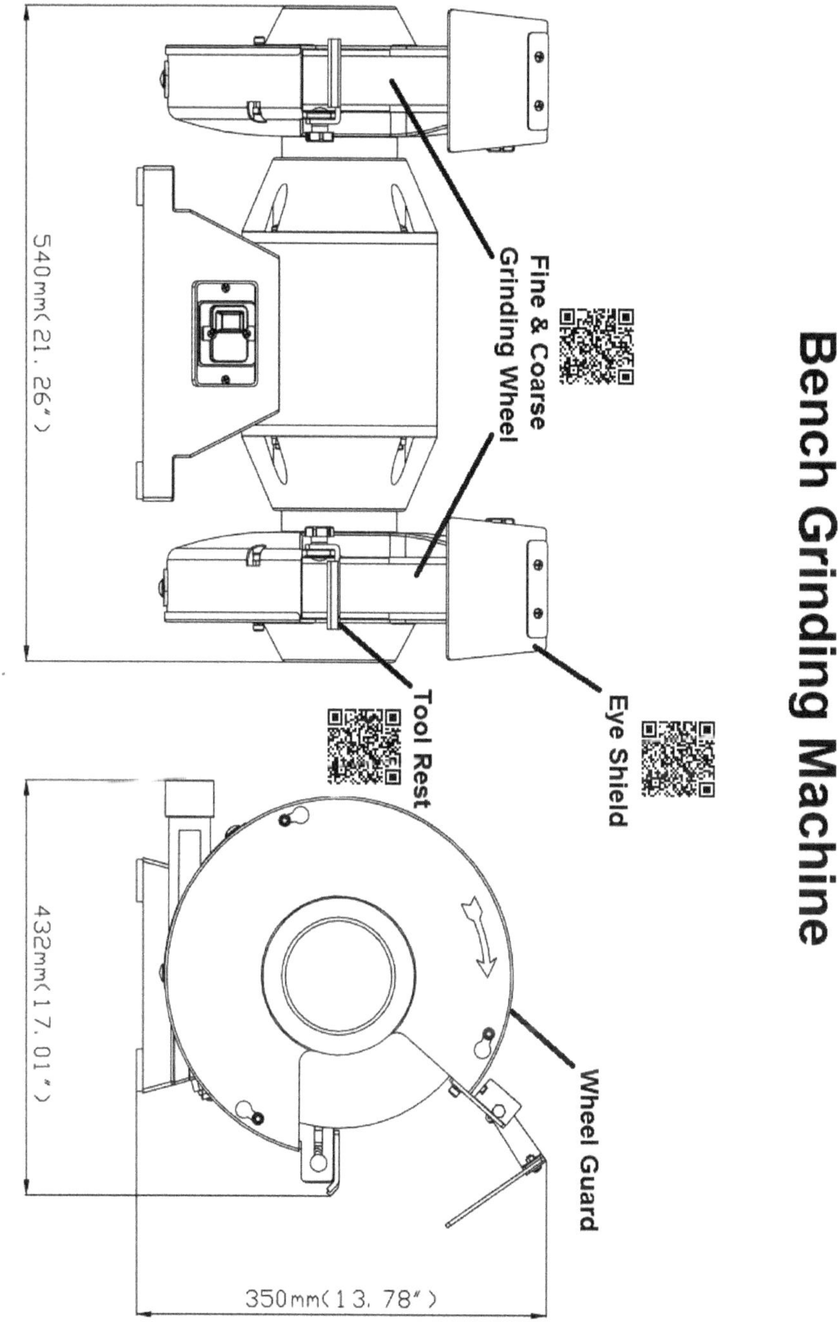

# Bench Grinding Machine



Bench Grinding Machine

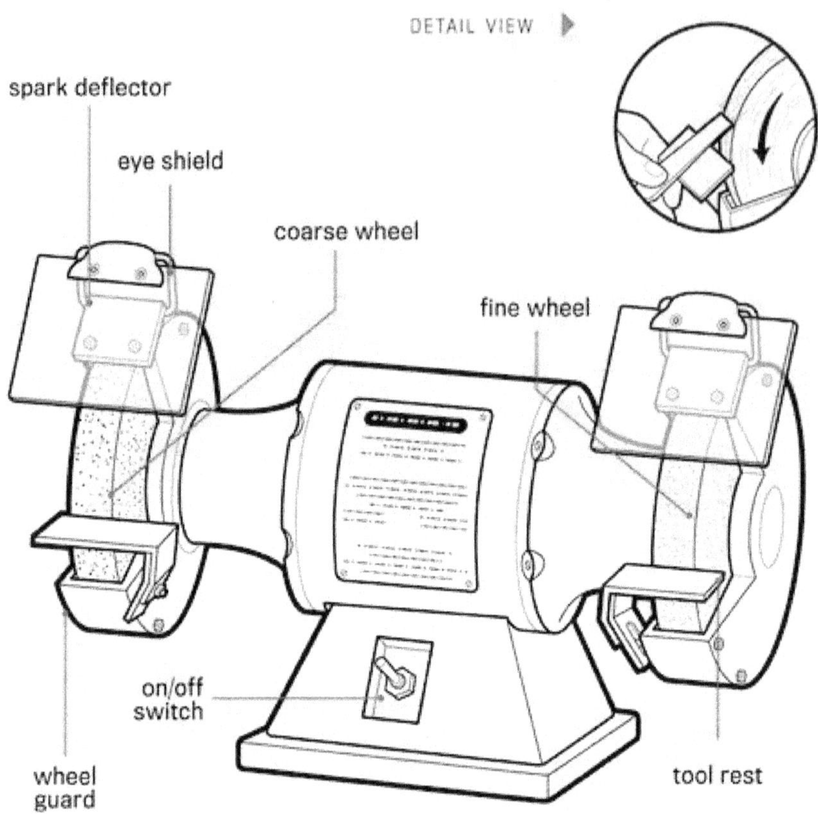


Bench Grinding Machine 1

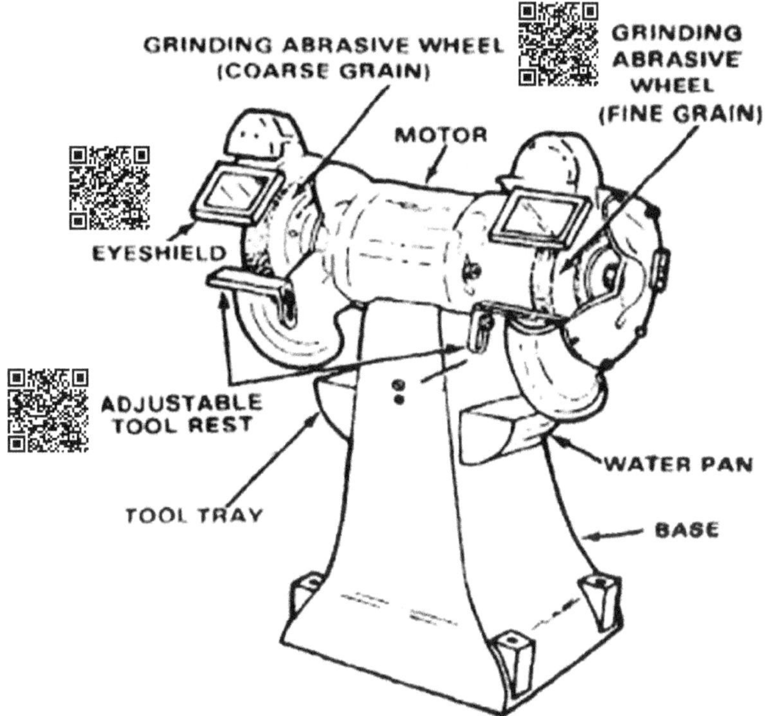


# Pedastal Grinding Machine

Pedastal Grinding Machine

# CHAPTER TWO

# Turner First Year MCQ

01] In case of bleeding, take treatment Of

A] spray cold water

B] Bandage immediately -----]

C] Enquire about the accident thought treatment

D] cold 3" and rest

02] in case of an accident, the victim should im

A] Asked to take rest

C] Attended immediately

D] leave him

03] First aid is given to an injured or ill person primarily....

A] Save life

B] Prevent further deterioration of the muff's

C] Give best possible comfort

D] All of these

04] Colour code for Bins for waste paper segregation is -----

A] blue Colour

B] Yellow Colour

C] Red Colour

D] Green Colour

05] In Japanese Seiko stands for --------------

A] Shine

B] Sort

C] Standardize

D] Sustain

06] Benefit of SS system is ------

A] Increase in productivity

B] Increase in quality

C] Reduction in wastage of time

D] All of these

07] Safety is -----------

A] nobody's business

B] every bodise business

C] Some bodies business

D] The organization business

08] For basic categories of safety signs are available The meaning of"prohibition" sign ----

A] shows it must not be done

B] Shows what must be done

C] Warns the hazard or danger

D] Gives information of safety provision

09] Which one is a workshop safety?

A] Keep shop floor clean and free from grease, oil or other slippery materials

B] Stop the machine before changing the speed

C] Don't use cracked or chipped tools

D] Don't try to stop a running machine with hand

10] In Personal Protect Equipment (PPE] HELMET is used to

A] protect head

B] Protect eyes

C] Protcct haııds

D] Protect ears

11] Which of the following belongs to general safety?

A Have a worker in good attitude

B] The work clean and clear

C] Concentrate on your work

D] Keep the floor and gangways clean and clear

12] While grinding, which is used to protect the eyes?

A] Dark green glass

B] Mask

C] Sun glasses

D] Safety goggles

13] Which of the following is done for machine safety?

A] Check the oil level before starting the machine

B] Do things in a methodical way

C] Keep the floor and gangways clean and clear

D] Don't use dies and scarves

14] ln Personal Protect Equipment (PPE], 'sleeves' is used to protect ----------

A] Face
B] Eyes
C] Ears
D] Hands
15] ABC stands for --------------
A] Automatic Breathing Control
B] Automatic Blood Control
C] Airway Breathing Circulation
D] Automatic Blood Circulation
16] To put off"Class B" fire, the types of fire extinguisher used is ...........]
A] dry power
B] Carbon dioxide
C] Jet of water
D] Foam type
17] Which type of fire extinguisher is used to put off general fire?
A] Water type Extinguisher
B] Foam type Extinguisher
C] Dry chemical powder Extinguisher
D] Carbon dioxide (C02] Extinguisher
18] One micrometer (U] is equal to...
A] 0.1mm
B] 0.01mm
C] 0.001mm
D] 0.0001mm
19] Name the tool used to make and finish the leak proof joints of a pipe T joint
A] groover
B] setting hammer
C] creasing hammer
D] round bottom stake
20] Portion of the hammer used for fixing the handle is...
A] Face
B] Peen
C] Cheek
D] Eye hole
21] Weight of the hammer for the marking purpose is...

A] <u>250g</u>

B] 500g

C] 1 kg

D] 2 kgs

22] To cut out small apertures which punch and die type of machine is used?

A] shear type nibbler

B] <u>punch type nibbler</u>

C] circular cutting machine

D] guillotine shearing machine

23] Scribers are made of...

A] Mild steel

B] <u>High carbon steel</u>

C] Brass

D] Cast iron

24] The size of an engineer's vice is specified by the...

A] Length of the movable jaw

B] <u>Width of the jaws</u>

C] Height of the vice

D] Maximum opening of the jaws

Bench Vice Animation & Video

25] The form of thread used in carpenters vice is...

A] Square

B] Acme thread

C] <u>Sawtooth Thread</u>

D] Knuckle thread

26] The convexity of files helps...

A] To file concave surfaces

B] To file convex surfaces

C] <u>To prevent rounding of edges of work</u>

D] The file to become straight when pressure is applied

27]] Name the instrument used to check the perpendicularity of the branch pipe with the main pipe of a pipe T joint

A] protractor

B] <u>try square</u>

C] spirit level

D] straight edge

28] The caliper meant for measuring the width of a slot is...

A] Odd leg caliper

B] Outside caliper

C] Jenny caliper

D] <u>Inside calliper</u>

29] The included angle of the groove of 'V' block is always....

A] 45°

B] 60°

C] 90°

D] <u>120°</u>

'V' blocks Animation & Video

30] 'V' blocks are available in grades of...

A] <u>A & B</u>

B] A,B & C

C] 1,2 & 3

D] 1 & 2

31] 'V' blocks of grade 'B' are made of

A] <u>Cast iron</u>

B] Mild steel

C] Steel

D] Cast steel

32] 'V' block 50/5-40 A is used for holding jobs of diameter

A] Ø 50 mm

B] Ø 5 to Ø 50 mm

C] <u>Ø 5 to Ø 40 mm</u>

D] Ø 40 mm

33] The reason for using cast iron in making 'V' blocks

A] to increase the weight of the block

B] to reduce the cost

C] <u>to reduce the friction</u>

D] to get a good appearance

34] For cutting thin tubing, the most suitable pitch of the hacksaw blade is...

A] 1.8mm

B] 1.4mm

C] 1mm

D] <u>0.8mm</u>

35] For cutting solid brass, the most suitable pitch of the hacksaw blade is...

A] <u>1.8mm</u>

B] 1.4mm

C] 1mm

D] 0.8mm

36] A new hacksaw blade after a few strokes becomes loose because of the...

A] <u>Stretching of the blade</u>

B] Wing-nut threads being worn out

C] Wrong pitch of the blade

D] Improper selection of the set of saws.

37] While cutting small diameter pipes, it is advisable to watch regularly and ensure that...

A] The cut is along the curved line

B] <u>More saw teeth are in contract</u>

C] The work is not overheated

D] Proper balancing of hacksaw is maintained

38] If the drill runs untrue, it will

A] get too hot

B] cut undersize

C] distort the spindle

D] <u>cut an oversized hole</u>

39] Running the drill too fast many result in

A] <u>spoiling the cutting edge</u>

B] poor surface finish

C] twisting the tang

D] drilling an oval hole

40] A drill with worn land will

A] drill hole oversize

B] <u>drill hole undersize</u>

C] run out of centre

D] drill an accurate hole

41] The morse taper provided on drills used on lathe ranges between

A] <u>MT1 to MT5</u>

B] MT1 to MT4

C] MT0 to MT5

D] MT0 to MT4

42] Feeding the small drill too fast into the work may result in

A] <u>breaking the drill</u>

B] bending the drill

C] cutting an oval shape hole

D] increased production

43] The drill size for a M 20 tap is

A] <u>17.5 mm</u>

B] 18 mm

C] 18.5 mm

D] 19 mm

44] The taper shank drills are held on the machine by means of…

A] Chucks

B] <u>Sleeves</u>

C] Drift

D] Vice

45] Drill chucks are fitted on the drilling machine spindle by means of a…

A] Knurled ring

B] <u>Arbor</u>

C] Drift

D] Pinion and key

Drill Chuck Animation & Video

46] The Morse taper provided on drills ranges between…

A] <u>MT 1 to MT 5</u>

B] MT 1 to MT 4

C] MT 0 to MT 5

D] MT 0 to MT 4

47] A drift is used for…

A] Drawing a drill location

B] Fixing chuck on the machine spindle

C] Removing a broken drill from the work

D] <u>Removing the drill from the machine spindle</u>

48] When the taper shank of the drill is larger than the machine spindle, the device to hold the drill is a…

A] Drill sleeve

B] <u>Taper socket</u>

C] Drill drift

D] Chuck and key

49] A special feature of the radial drilling machine is…

A] It can be used for drilling with a H.S.S] drill

B] Table can be moved and set at any position

C] A variety of speeds is available

D] <u>The spindle can be brought to any position</u>

50] The point angle of drills depends on...

A] The size of the drill

B] The type of machine

C] <u>The material of the work</u>

D] The RPM of the drill

51] The point angle for a standard drill is...

A] 60°

B] 108°

C] <u>118°</u>

D] 135°

52] The helical angle determines the...

A] Cutting angle

B] Chew angle

C] <u>Rake angle</u>

D] Lip angle

53] The clearance angle of the drill is between...

A] 3° to 5°

B] <u>8° to 12°</u>

C] 12° to 20°

D] 15° to 20°

54] The relief angle provided behind the cutting edge is called the..

A] Point angle

B] Chisel edge angle

C] Helix angle

D] <u>Clearance angle</u>

55] A set of number drill series consists of drills in the following ranges] Indicate the correct range

A] 1 to 40

B] 1 to 50

C] <u>1 to 80</u>

D] 1 to 100

56] In the number drill series, the smallest drill size is...

A] 0.1 mm

B] <u>0.35 mm</u>

C] 0.5 mm
D] 0.52 mm
57] In the number drill series, the largest drill size is...
A] 102 mm
B] 5.791 mm
C] 5.613 mm
D] 5.410 mm
58] In the letter drill series, the size of the drill 'A' is equal to ...
A] 13 mm
B] 6.08 mm
C] 6.045 mm
D] 5.944 mm
59] In the letter drill series, the largest drill size is equal to...
A] 10.33 mm
B] 10.490 mm
C] 12.01 mm
D] 15.00 mm
60] In a remote place ( no electricity available] a rail track is to be drilled] Choose the right drilling machine
A] Radial drilling machine
B] Pillar drilling machine
C] Ratchet drilling machine
D] Sensitive drilling Machine
61] A drilling machine used by a carpenter for cabinet making is a...
A] Ratchet drilling machine
B] Radial drilling machine
C] Breast drilling machine
D] Sensitive drilling machine
62] Surface plates are made of...
A] High grade cast steel
B] Fine-grained cast iron
C] Alloy steels
D] Wrought iron
63] The drill size for a M 20 tap is
A] 17.5 mm
B] 18 mm
C] 18.5 mm
D] 19 mm

64] Tapping is mostly done to produce
A] external 'V' thread
B] <u>internal 'V' thread</u>
C] external square thread
D] internal square thread
65] The drill size for tapping is
A] more than the tap size
B] <u>less than the tap size</u>
C] equal to the tap size
D] either more or less than the tap size
66] which one of the following is the most suitable tap for lathe work?
A] spiral tap
B] <u>machine tap</u>
C] hand tap
D] left hand tap
67] A die is turned with a
A] die wrench
B] <u>diestock</u>
C] die plate
D] die handle
68] A tumbler gear unit has
A] a single gear
B] two gears
C] <u>three gears</u>
D] four gears
69] The cutting edge of a solid tool is made of
A] <u>carbon steel</u>
B] mild steel
C] super high speed steel
D] stelite
70] The tip of a cemented carbide threading tool is
A] <u>brazed</u>
B] welded
C] soldered
D] clamped to the shank
71] Tool will rub against the work surfaces and the cutting force increases when..
A] The clearance angle is more

B] <u>The clearance angel is less</u>
C] The rake angle is more
D] The rake angle is less
72] Formation of a chip while cutting is based on the...
A] <u>Rake angle of the tool</u>
B] Clearance angle of the tool
C] Wedge angle of the tool
D] Clearance and wedge angle of the tool
73] The suitable cutting fluid for drilling mild steel in a drilling machine
is...
A] Synthetic soluble oil
B] Neat oil
C] Distilled water
D] <u>Soluble oil</u>
74] Centre drilling is an operation of...
A] <u>Drilling and countersinking</u>
B] Drilling and counter boring
C] Marking the centre location before drilling
D] Enlarging the diameter of a hole
75] Shaft ends are centre drilled for...
A] <u>Supporting jobs between centres</u>
B] Lubricating the dead centre
C] Reducing the weight
D] Assisting counter boring
76] The Centre drill size is selected on the basis of the
A] length of the job
B] material of the job
C] <u>diameter of the job</u>
D] type of operation
77] Centre drilling is done at a
A] high spindle speed with a high feed
B] low spindle speed with a high feed
C] <u>high spindle speed with a low feed</u>
D] low spindle speed with a low feed
78] The least count of vernier caliper is
A] 0.01 mm
B] <u>0.02mm</u>
C] 0.001 mm

D] 0.2 mm

Vernier Caliper Animation & Video

79] The graduations of a depth micrometer are...

A] Similar to an outside micrometer

B] <u>In the reverse direction to that of the outside micrometer, both Thimble and sleeve</u>

C] In the reverse direction only on the sleeve

D] In the direction only on the thimble

Depth Micrometer Animation & Video

80] The process of enlarging the end of a hole for accommodating the socket screw head is...

A] Reaming

B] Spot facing

C] <u>Counter boring</u>

D] Counter sinking

Boring Operation

81]While choosing a boring tool for boring a given diameter, select

A] a long tool

B] a short tool

C] a long and stout tool

D] <u>a short and stout tool</u>

82] The cutting edge of the boring tool should be set for a small hole so that it is

A] 0.5 mm above the center

B] 0.5 mm below the center

C] 1 mm above the center

D] <u>in the exact center</u>

83] Bored holes are to be chamfered by using

A] a drill

B] triangular scraper

C] <u>a cranked boring tool</u>

D] a flat file

84] The tool used for boring deep holes is a

A] lathe mandrel

B] sleeve

C] drill

D] boring bar

E] <u>auger bit</u>

85] The cutting speed for rough boring is the
A] same as rough turning
B] same as drilling
C] same as knurling
D] same as thread cutting
86] The reamer is used for...
A] Drilling holes in thin sheets
B] Drilling deep holes
C] Removing burrs
D] Enlarging and finishing holes

Reamer Animation & Video

87] The reamer teeth are unevenly spaced because...
A] They are easy to manufacture
B] They can reduce chattering
C] They help to cut metal gradually
D] They help to remove the reamer easily
88] Which among the following is not a capability of reamers?
A] Finishing small holes
B] Finishing any machined profiles
C] Accuracy to closer limits
D] Producing high quality surface finish
89] The most important quality of any cutting fluid is
A] emulsification
B] specific heat
C] specific gravity
D] viscosity

Cutting Fluid

90] By using coolants on workpieces we can choose
A] higher cutting speeds
B] lower cutting feeds
C] lower cutting speeds
D] heavy depth of cuts
91] The cutting speed for aluminium with H.S.S] tools is
A] 30 m/min
B] 50 m/min
C] 70 m/min
D] 130 m/min
92] The cutting speed for brass with a H.S.S] tool is

A] 10 m/min

B] 25 m/min

C] 70 m/min

D] 140 m/min

93] The distance, which the cutting edge of a tool passes over the material in a minute while machining is Know as...

A] RPM

B] Feed

C] Machine speed

D] Cutting speed

94] The cutting angle for chipping cast iron is...

A] 37.5°

B] 55°

C] 60°

D] 90°

95] The depth of cut is given by

A] the top slide

B] the cross-slide

C] the compound slide

D] adjusting the tool

96] For mounting a lathe chuck

A] start it by hand and then turn the power on

B] mount it on by power

C] mount it by hand

D] mount it with the help of a hammer

Lathe Four Jaw Chuck Animation & Video

97] The morse taper provided on drills used on lathe ranges between

A] MT1 to MT5

B] MT1 to MT4

C] MT0 to MT5

D] MT0 to MT4

98] Feeding the small drill too fast into the work may result in

A] breaking the drill

B] bending the drill

C] cutting an oval shape hole

D] increased production

99] Number of flutes in a twist drills are --------

A] 1

B] 2

C] 3

D] 4

100] Which one of the following drilling machines is used for drilling holes where electricity is not available?

A] Bench drilling machine

B] Pillar drilling machine

C] Redial drilling machine

D] Ratchet drilling machine

101] Which one of the following drilling machine is used for heavy duty work?

A] Bench drilling machine

B] Pillar drilling machine

C] Radial drilling machine

D] Electric hand drilling machine

102] The suitable cutting fluid for drilling mild steel in a lathe is

A] synthetic soluble oil

B] neat cutting oil

C] distilled water

D] soluble oil+water

103] The suitable cutting fluid for precision grinding is

A] Soluble oil

B] Synthetic soluble oil

C] Neat oil

D] Servo Cut's'

Grinding Wheel Animation & Video

104] Advantage of using cutting fluid during grinding operation is ------

A] 5000 surface finish

B] Reduction in cutting forces

C] Reduction in hardening of the work piece

D] All of these]

105] Lubricant is necessary to ...........]

A] run the machine smoothly taking least load

B] Run the machine quickly

C] Stop the machine immediately

D] Produce work piece of greater accuracy

106] The main purpose for using a lubricant in machine tools is to ------

A] Cool down the making parts

B] Prevent machine tool from heating

C] Wet the making parts for close contact

D] Minimize the friction between the making parts

107] Driving plates are used for

A] mounting fixtures and workpieces

B] driving shafts between Centre's with a lathe dog

C] facing operations only

D] internal operations only

108] Balancing is done in the face plate work

A] to increase the speed

B] to reduce the pressure on the tool

C] for uniform rotation of work

D] to get a good finish

109] A face plate is used to hold

A] a round job

B] a finished job

C] an irregular Job

D] a hollow job

110] Which is correct angle plate used with face plate

(A] Solid Type

(B] Box Type

(C] Adjustable Type

(D] None of them

Angle Plate Animation & Video

111] Face plate is made from.....]

(A] Mild Steel

(B] Cast Iron

(C] Brass

(D] Aluminium

112] Which following accessories is use for odd an uneven job turning?

(A] Three Jaw Chuck

(B] Two Jaw Chuck

(C] Driving Plate

(D] Face Plate

113] An irregular shaped work piece is turned on a Lathe] Which one of the following work holding accessories is used?

A] Two Jaw chuck

B] Three Jaw chuck

C] Driving plate
D] Face plate
114]The pads of a steady rest are made of
A] carbon steel
B] lead
C] mild steel
D] brass

Steady Rest Animation & Video

115] A steady rest is used
A] to hold jobs
B] for face plate work
C] to drive the job
D] to support the job
116] A follower steady is held on the
A] lathe bed
B] lathe carriage
C] lathe spindle
D] tailstock
117] When turning long work pieces, the following is used
A sleeve
B change gear
C steady rest
D bracket]
118] Knurling operation is done at the
A] turning spindle speed
B] high spindle speed
C] 1/3 of the turning spindle speed
D] 1/2 of the turning spindle speed

Knurling Tool Animation & Video

119] Knurling is the operation of
A] shearing
B] forming
C] turning
D] pressing
120] Mandrels are generally used when machining with
A] heavy cuts
B] short facing cuts
C] light cuts

D] boring tools

121] In the B.I.S system 25 hole deviations are specified by

A] small letters

B] small letters with numbers

C] small letters with tolerance

D] <u>capital letters</u>

122] The standard range of sizes covered in the B.I.S] system of limits and fits are

A] 0 to 10 mm

B] 0 to 100 mm

C] <u>25 to 400 mm</u>

D] 0 to 500 mm

123] The basic size is the size

A] mentioned in the drawing

B] machined by the operator

C] <u>based on which deviations are given</u>

D] given by the instructor

124] Limits of size are

A] <u>2</u>

B] 3

C] 4

D] 5

125] The number of fundamental deviations in the B.I.S] system are

A] 20

B] 22

C] <u>25</u>

D] 28

126] The number of grade of tolerances in the B.I.S] system are

A] 12

B] <u>16</u>

C] 18

D] 20

127] The size based on which the dimensional deviations are given is called...

A] Actual size

B] <u>Basic size</u>

C] Minimum limit of size

D] Maximum limit of Size

128] The size of parts made by .....] for provide interchange ability properties] (A] Measurement System

(B] Trial and Error System

(C] Limit and Tolerance System

(D] None of Them

129] Your job taper is correct if it is measured

A above the higher limit

B in between higher and lower limit

C below the lower limit]

130] When tolerance given in one side of the basic dimension, it is called ---------

A].Tolerance system

B] Unilateral tolerance

C] Bilateral tolerance

D] Allowance System

131] A dimension is stated as (025 H7 in a drawing] The lower limit is -----------

A] 24.75 mm

B] 24.85 mm

C] 25.00 mm

D] 25-021 mm

132] The measured Size Of the dimensions of a component as called---------

A] Basic size

B] Nominal Size

C] Allowed size

D] Actual size

133] In the drawing the dimensions of a shaft is shown 40i 0068/0042, which is the size of Shaft within the tolerance?

A] 4.0.64 mm

B] 40.042 mm

C] 40.000 mm

D] 39.998 mm

134] In Hole basic system ----------

A] The size of the shaft is made constant

B] The Size of the hole is made constant

C] Only 'allowance is given on the hole

D] The permissible tolerance are given on the hole and the Shaft

135] The Size of a component is given as 24 -0.1] What does -O.1 indicates? _

A] Upper deviation is + 0.1 mm ]

B] Lower deviation is 0.0 mm

C] Fundamental deviation is 0.0 mm

D] Lower deviation is _0.1 mm

136] The tolerance of a hole iS the difference between the -------

A] Maximum hole Size and maximum Shaft size

B] Maximum hole size and maximum hole Size

C] Minimum'hole size and maximum Shaft Size

D] Minimum hole Size and minimum shaft Size

137] A hole whose lower deviation is zero is called basic hole] Which one of the following letter indicates basic hole? ]

A] E

B] F

C] G '

D] H

138] Which one having upper deviation zero?

A] Bassc Shaft

B] Basic hole

C] Tolerance

D] Clearance

139] A ball bearing on a shaft is type of fit? ,

A] Clearance fit

B] Driving fit

C] Shrinkage fit

D] None of the above

140] Which one of the following is important factor required to achieve the interchange ability in mass production? ]

A] Geometrical accuracy]

B] Standardization

C] Dimensional accuracy

D] Surface finish

141] In the BIS system of limits and fits, the grade of tolerance are represented by number Symbols and there are ---------i

A] 14 grades of tolerance

B] 16 grades of tolerance

C] 18 grades of tolerance '

D] 20 grades of tolerance

142] A Product is said to have the quality when ..........]

A] Its shape and dimensions are within the limit

B] It is fit for use

C] It appears to be very good

D] The choice of material is right

143] The maximum clearance required between hole'30 +0.021, 0.000 and shaft 30 -0.110, 0.143 is.

A] 0.110 mm '

B] 0.131 mm

C] 0.164 mm

D] 0.143 mm

144] A dimension is stated as 25 .1002 mm in a drawing] What is the tolerance?

A] +0.02 mm'

B] +0.04 mm

C] -0.02 mm

D] 25.00 mm

145] A pin is fitted in a hole] The tolerance zone of the pin is entirely above that of hole] The fit obtained will be?

A] Clearance fit

B] Transition fit

C] Interference fit

D] Running fit

146] Interchange ability is normally applied for? _

A] Repairing of parts

B] Mass production

C] Single piece production

D] All of these

147] Tolerance is given to the part size to..........]

A] Production the part within the required permissible size error

B] Increase the production

C] Decrease the Production

D] Finish the components approximately

148] Which one of the following is the clearance fit under the whole basic system?

A] 20 H7/p6'

B] 2067/211

C] ZOG/gll ]

D] 20H/g11]

149] The three classes of fits as per BIS system aré ...........] ~ ]

A] Clearance fit, interference fit and transition fit

B] Medium fit, push fit and tight fit

C] Flat fit, round fit and square fit

D] 'Sliding fit ', loose fit and shrinkage fit

150] Which one of the following tolerance specifications has a maximum dimensionless than 20 mm?

A] 20 +0.2,-0.3

B] 20 320.2

C] 20 -0.2, 0.3 e

D]m 20 +500, ~03

151] Difference between the maximum and minimum limit is -~-~~~~-~~~~~ '

A] Single informant

B] Basic shaft

C] Clearance

D] Tolerance

152] A shaft 55 running freely in bush bearing the type of fit is ---------

A] Clearance fit

B] Driving plate

C] shrinkage fit

D] None of the above

153] The taper ratio of the morse taper is

A] 1 in 10

B] 1 in 15

C] 1 in 20

D] 1 in 25

154] The morse standard taper is available in

A] 16 Nos

B] 12 Nos

C] 10 Nos

D] 8 Nos

155] Taper turning by offsetting the tailstock method can produce

A] an internal taper

B] an internal taper thread

C] an external taper

D] both external and internal tapers

Taper by Tailstock Offset Animation & Video

156] By using the taper turning attachment, tapers can be turned with a setting angle up to

A] 10°

B] <u>15°</u>

C] 20°

D] 30°

157] The accuracy of a taper is generally checked by means of......

A] <u>taper gauges</u>

B] gauge blocks

C] indicator and height gauge

D] 'V' blocks

158] Turning tapers by the compound rest method involves working solely with

Decimal measurements

B fractional measurements

C metric measurements

<u>D angular measurements]</u>

159] Long tapers are produced

A with the taper turning attachment

B with the compound slide

<u>C by setting over the tail stock</u>

D by adjusting the cross slide]

160] The length of turned tapers are checked with

<u>A vernier calliper</u>

B micrometer

C inside callper

D dial test indicator]

161] The disadvantages of taper turning using the com] pound slide are

A] only long tapers can be turned

B] only very large tapers can be turned

C] only manual in feed is possible

<u>D] only short tapers can be turned due to the restrictions of the compound slide]</u>

162] External tapers are checked with

A] limit plug gauge

<u>B] taper ring gauge</u>

C ]taper plug gauge

D] thread plug gauge]

163] The use of a taper turned on lathe is ----

A] Assist to transmit drive in the assembled parts

B] Used for Assembly and disassembly of parts

C] Give self alignment in the assembled parts

164] Which type of method is used in mass production of production of producing small length of taper?

A] Form tool

B] Compound slide

C] Tailstock offset.

D] Taper turning attachment

165] Morse standard taper is one of the internationally accepted standards taper, which is available in numbers from--------

A]1to7

B]1 to 8

C] O to 7

D] 0 to 8

166] Which taper turning method is used for cutting steep taper?

A] Set over method

B] Taper turning attachment

C] Form tool

D] Swivelling the compound rest

167] Morse taper is used in which of the following machine components -...

A] Spindles of lathe

B] Spindles of drill machine

C] Shanks of reamers

D] All of these

168] For mass production of the taper which one of the following method is used.......]

A] Tailstock offset method

B] Taper turning attachment method

C] Form too method

D] Compound slide method

169] The major diameter of the taper is 40 mm, minor diameter is 30 mm] The total length of the job is 100 mm is tapered then offset is given by -

A] 5 mm
B] 7.5 mm
C] 12 mm
D] 9 mm
170] The accuracy of an ordinary bevel protractor is --' ------------degree]
A] One
B] Three
C] Two
D] Four
171] The least count of a vernier bevel protractor is...
A] 1"
B] 5'
C] 1°
D] 5 °
172] The part of a vernier bevel protractor which is normally used as a reference base for measuring angles is the...
A] Blade
B] Stock
C] Disc
C] Main scale
173] The part of a vernier bevel protector on which main scale divisions are marked is the...
A] Stock
B] Dial
C] Disc
D] Adjustable blade
174] The part of a bevel protractor, which comes in contact with the inclined surface while measuring is the...
A] Blade
B] Stock
C] Disc
D] Dial
175] The value of each division of the main scale of a vernier bevel protractor is...
A] 5'
B] 1°
C] 5°

D.10∘

176] The value of each division of the vernier scale of a bevel protractor is...

A] 1∘

B] 1∘5'

C] <u>1∘55'</u>

D.5'

177] The part of the vernier bevel protractor on which main scale divisions are marked

A stock

<u>B dial</u>

C disc

D adjustable blade

178] In Vernier bevel protractor is designed to measure?

A] Acute angles

B] Obtuse angles

C] <u>Acute and Obtuse angle</u>

D] Liner dimensions

179] To get least count of 5 in a vernier bevel protractor the 23° main scale are divided into -..

A] <u>12 equal parts on vernier scale</u>

B] 22 equal parts on vernier scale

C] 24 equal parts on vernier scale

D] 25 equal parts on vernier scale

180] Which of the following is not the part of a combination set?

A] <u>Stock</u>

B] Square head

C] Protractor head

D] Centre head

181] The datum, form which the measurements of the vernier height gauge are taken, is...

A] The beam

B] The vernier slide

C] <u>The base</u>

D] Above the scriber poing

Vernier Height Gauge Animation & Video

182]The part of a vernier height gauge on which the main scale divisions are graduated is the...

A] Base

B] <u>Beam</u>

C] Fine setting device

D] The vernier plate

183] On which part of the vernier height gauge are the main scale division graduated? ]

A] Base

B] Vernier plate

C] <u>Beam</u>

D] Fine adjusting unit

184] For marking purpose a Vernier height gauge must be on the --------

A] Bed of a machine tool

B] <u>Surface plate</u>

C] Square block

D] Any flat surface

185] Before using Vernier height gauge make sure that the --------

A] Locking screw is in a locked position

B] Scriber is Locked

C] <u>Zero of the vernier coincides with zero of the main scale</u>

D] Gib is Provided

186] The least count Of a vernier height gauge is...........]

A] 0.05 mm

B] 0.1 mm

C] <u>0.02 mm</u>

D] 0001 mm

187] Which laying out the vernier height gauge must be used on the ----------

A] V block

B] Machine bed

C] <u>Surface plate</u>

D] Any flat surface

188] The part which is slides on the beam of a vernier height gauge is known as a ------

A] Base

B] Beam scale

C] Scriber

D] <u>Vernier slide</u>

189] The base of the vernier height gauge is generally made out of ----------

A] Cast iron]

B] Steel

C] Aluminium alloy

D] Tungsten carbide

190] Which instrument iis used for marking layout?

A] Micrometer

B] Vernier

C] Depth gauge

D] Vernier height gauge

191] While marking with a Vernier height gauge, the work piece is generally ----------

A] Supported by an angle plate

B] Supported by another work piece

C] Held by one hand

D] Held without support

192] Which of the following is not the part of a combination set?

A] Stock

B] Square head

C] Protractor head

D] Centre head

193] A BSW threading tool is to be ground with an included angle of

A] 55°

B] 60°

C] 47.5°

D] 29°

194] The nose radius of a metric 'V' thread tool is

A] 0.144 x P

B] 0.25 x P

C] 0.414 x P

D] 0.0144 x P

195] While cutting metric external threads of coarse pitches, it is advisable to swivel the compound rest to

A] 45°

B] 30°

C] 60°

D.90°
196] The depth of B.I.S] metric thread is
A] 0.6403 x P
B] 0.6 x P
C] 0.6134 x P
D] 0.5 x P
197] Threading tools are checked for accuracy for the 60° angle by using
a
A] Thread plug gauge
B] centre gauge
C] screw pitch gauge
D] tool angle gauge
198] The number of threads per inch can be checked with a
A] tool gauge
B] metric rule by counting
C] ring gauge
D] screw pitch gauge
199] When threading, the carriage is moved along the ways by
A] a gear train on a track
B] the feed rod spline or key-way
C] the lead screw thred
D] the hand wheel
200] Thread chasers are used for
A] quick production of threads
B] maintaining an exact form of thread
C] cutting threads on hard materials
D] cutting threads on soft materials
Thread Chasers Animation & Video
201] Thread chasers are made out of
A] carbon steel
B] high speed steel
C] tool used
D] stainless steel
202] Chasers are used to cut
A] 'V' form threads only
B] square threads only
C] acme threads only
D] any form of threads

203] To cut M24 x 3 mm pitch internal threads, the core diameter of the job is

A] 27.00 mm

B] 24.50 mm

C] <u>21.00 mm</u>

D] 24.00 mm

204] The depth of cut for M24 x 3 mm internal thread is

A] <u>0.5412 x 3</u>

B] 0.6134 x 3

C] 0.5 x 3

D] 0.7 x 3

205] To cut 24 x 3 mm internal acme threads, the core diameter of the job is

A] 20.00 mm

B] 21.66 mm

C] 21.00 mm

D] <u>20.60 mm</u>

206] The depth of cut for metric square threading is

A] 0.6 x P

B] <u>0.5 x P</u>

C] 0.5412 x P

D] 0.6412 x P

207] To cut buttress thread, the depth of cut is

A] 0.5412 x P

B] <u>0.6 x P</u>

C] 0.7 x P

D] 0.75 x P

208] For cutting acme threads, the tool is ground to an included angle of

A] 60°

B] 29°

C] <u>47.5°</u>

D] 30°

209] The half-nut lever is used for

A] engaging the longitudinal feed on the carriage

B] taking up the slack in the cross-slide nut

C] changing from longitudinal to cross-feed

D] <u>threads cutting</u>

210] The bottom surface joining the two sides of adjacent thread ( external thread ] is...

A] Flank

B] <u>Root</u>

C] Crest

D] Pitch

211] The form of thread used in carpenters vice is...

A] Square

B] Acme thread

C] <u>Sawtooth Thread</u>

D] Knuckle thread

212] What is the angle of pipe thread?

A 60°

B 47'/2°

C 29°

<u>D 55°]</u>

213] What is the use of pipe thread?

A transmission

B maintain pressure

<u>C airtight connections</u>

D none of the above]

214] What is the depth of the 2" pipe thread?

A 0.5"

B 0.640"

C 0.335"

<u>D 0.580"]</u>

215] External Thread provide on Rod or Pipe , by Die and Cutting Tool is called ......

(A] Tapping

(B] Dieing

<u>(C] Threading</u>

(D] Grooving

Threading Animation & Video

216] The angle 0f lS thread (V shaped] is ----------

A] 29°

B] 47 1/4°

C] 50°

<u>D] 60</u>

217] ln which of the following methods, only external threads are made --------

A] Form tool mEthOd

B] Compound rest method

C] Tailstock offset method

D] Taper turning attachment method]

218] The surface joining the crest and the root of a thread is known as ----

A] Flank

B] Shank

C] Pitch surface

D] All Of these

219] Pitch of a two start thread is 4 mm] Then the lead of the thread is given by -----

A] 4mm

B] 2mm

C] 8mm

D] 6mm

220] The Gear ratio required for cutting a screw thread of 2.5 mm on a lathe having a lead screw pitch using single point cutting tool is ----

A] 1:2

B] 2:1

C] 1:1 mm

221] Soft soldering is done

A] below 450° C

B] above 450°C

C] at 900°C

D] above 1000°C

222] Brazing is done

A] at 1900°C

B] above 450°C

C] at 1000°C

D] below 450°C

223] A brazed joint is

A] weaker than a soldered joint

B] stronger than a solder join

C] stronger than a welded joint

D] weaker than a silver soldered joint
224] Ammonium chloride is used as a flux for soldering...
A] steel
B] aluminium
C] galvanized iron
D] stainless steel
225] Soldering of M.S sheets takes place at a temperature of...
A] 150◦C
B] 250◦C
C] 400◦C
D] 850◦C
226] In soldering operation the base metal is...
A] not heated
B] heated to 200◦C
C] heated to 650◦C
D] heated to red hot condition
227] Forge welding is classified as...
A] fusion welding without pressure
B] fusion welding with pressure
C] non-fusion welding without pressure
D] no-fusion welding with pressure
228] The selection of nozzle for pipe welding depends upon...
A] groove angle
B] welding position
C] pipe wall thickness
D] diameter of pipe
229] Name the flux used for brazing of M.S] sheets
A] hydrochloric acid
B] zinc chloride
C] tallow resin
D] borax
230] The depth of cut for M24 x 3 mm internal thread is
A] 0.5412 x 3
B] 0.6134 x 3
C] 0.5 x 3
D] 0.7 x 3

231] To cut 24 x 3 mm internal acme threads, the core diameter of the job is

A] 20.00 mm

B] 21.66 mm

C] 21.00 mm

D] <u>20.60 mm</u>

232] The depth of cut for metric square threading is

A] 0.6 x P

B] <u>0.5 x P</u>

C] 0.5412 x P

D] 0.6412 x P

233] To cut buttress thread, the depth of cut is

A] 0.5412 x P

B] <u>0.6 x P</u>

C] 0.7 x P

D] 0.75 x P

INDUSTRIAL TRAINING INSTITUTE

Monthly Test-1, Marks- 20, Date:- _______________

( Every Question Carry Two Marks )

**01] In case of bleeding, take treatment Of**

A] spray cold water

B] Bandage immediately -----]

C] Enquire about the accident thought treatment

D] cold 3" and rest

**02] in case of an accident, the victim should im**

A] Asked to take rest

C] Attended immediately

D] leave him

**03] First aid is given to an injured or ill person primarily....**

A] Save life

B] Prevent further deterioration of the muff's

C] Give best possible comfort

D] All of these

**04] Colour code for Bins for waste paper segregation is -----**

A] blue Colour

B] Yellow Colour

C] Red Colour

D] Green Colour

**05] In Japanese Seiko stands for --------------**

A] Shine

B] Sort

C] Standardize

D] Sustain

**06] Benefit of SS system is ------**

A] Increase in productivity

B] Increase in quality

C] Reduction in wastage of time

D] All of these

**07] Safety is -----------**

A] nobody's business

B] every bodise business

C] Some bodies business

D] The organization business

**08] For basic categories of safety signs are available The meaning of"prohibition" sign ----**

A] shows it must not be done

B] Shows what must be done

C] Warns the hazard or danger

D] Gives information of safety provision

**09] Which one is a workshop safety?**

A] Keep shop floor clean and free from grease, oil or other slippery materials

B] Stop the machine before changing the speed

C] Don't use cracked or chipped tools

D] Don't try to stop a running machine with hand

**10] In Personal Protect Equipment (PPE] HELMET is used to**

A] protect head

B] Protect eyes

C] Protect hands

D] Protect ears

INDUSTRIAL TRAINING INSTITUTE

Monthly Test-2, Marks- 20, Date:- ________________

( Every Question Carry Two Marks )

**1- 17] Which type of fire extinguisher is used to put off general fire?**

A] Water type Extinguisher

B] Foam type Extinguisher

C] Dry chemical powder Extinguisher

D] Carbon dioxide (C02] Extinguisher

**2-18] One micrometer (U] is equal to...**

A] 0.1mm

B] 0.01mm

C] 0.001mm

D] 0.0001mm

**3-19] Name the tool used to make and finish the leak proof joints of a pipe T joint**

A] groover

B] setting hammer

C] creasing hammer

D] round bottom stake

**4-20] Portion of the hammer used for fixing the handle is...**

A] Face

B] Peen

C] Cheek

D] Eye hole

**5-21] Weight of the hammer for the marking purpose is...**

A] 250g

B] 500g

C] 1 kg

D] 2 kgs

**6-22] To cut out small apertures which punch and die type of machine is used?**

A] shear type nibbler

B] punch type nibbler

C] circular cutting machine

D] guillotine shearing machine

**7-23] Scribers are made of...**

A] Mild steel

B] High carbon steel

C] Brass

D] Cast iron

**8-24] The size of an engineer's vice is specified by the...**

A] Length of the movable jaw

B] Width of the jaws

C] Height of the vice

D] Maximum opening of the jaws

**9-25] The form of thread used in carpenters vice is...**

A] Square

B] Acme thread

C] Sawtooth Thread

D] Knuckle thread

**10-26] The convexity of files helps...**

A] To file concave surfaces

B] To file convex surfaces

C] To prevent rounding of edges of work

D] The file to become straight when pressure is applied

INDUSTRIAL TRAINING INSTITUTE

Monthly Test-3, Marks- 20, Date:- ________________

( Every Question Carry Two Marks )

**1-33] The reason for using cast iron in making 'V' blocks**

A] to increase the weight of the block

B] to reduce the cost

C] to reduce the friction

D] to get a good appearance

**2-34] For cutting thin tubing, the most suitable pitch of the hacksaw blade is...**

A] 1.8mm

B] 1.4mm

C] 1mm

D] 0.8mm

**3-35] For cutting solid brass, the most suitable pitch of the hacksaw blade is...**

A] 1.8mm

B] 1.4mm

C] 1mm

D] 0.8mm

**4-36] A new hacksaw blade after a few strokes becomes loose because of the...**

A] Stretching of the blade

B] Wing-nut threads being worn out

C] Wrong pitch of the blade

D] Improper selection of the set of saws.

**5-37] While cutting small diameter pipes, it is advisable to watch regularly and ensure that...**

A] The cut is along the curved line

B] More saw teeth are in contract

C] The work is not overheated

D] Proper balancing of hacksaw is maintained

**6-38] If the drill runs untrue, it will**

A] get too hot

B] cut undersize

C] distort the spindle

D] cut an oversized hole

**7-39] Running the drill too fast many result in**

A] spoiling the cutting edge

B] poor surface finish

C] twisting the tang

D] drilling an oval hole

**8-40] A drill with worn land will**

A] drill hole oversize

B] drill hole undersize

C] run out of centre

D] drill an accurate hole

**9-41] The morse taper provided on drills used on lathe ranges between**

A] MT1 to MT5

B] MT1 to MT4

C] MT0 to MT5

D] MT0 to MT4

**10-42] Feeding the small drill too fast into the work may result in**

A] breaking the drill

B] bending the drill

C] cutting an oval shape hole

D] increased production

INDUSTRIAL TRAINING INSTITUTE

Monthly Test-4, Marks- 20, Date:- ________________

( Every Question Carry Two Marks )

**1-50] The point angle of drills depends on...**

A] The size of the drill

B] The type of machine

C] <u>The material of the work</u>

D] The RPM of the drill

**2-51] The point angle for a standard drill is...**

A] 60°

B] 108°

C] <u>118°</u>

D] 135°

**3-52] The helical angle determines the...**

A] Cutting angle

B] Chew angle

C] <u>Rake angle</u>

D] Lip angle

**4-53] The clearance angle of the drill is between...**

A] 3° to 5°

B] <u>8° to 12°</u>

C] 12° to 20°

D] 15° to 20°

**5-54] The relief angle provided behind the cutting edge is called the..**

A] Point angle

B] Chisel edge angle

C] Helix angle

D] <u>Clearance angle</u>

**6-55] A set of number drill series consists of drills in the following ranges] Indicate the correct range**

A] 1 to 40

B] 1 to 50

C] <u>1 to 80</u>

D] 1 to 100

**7-56] In the number drill series, the smallest drill size is...**

A] 0.1 mm

B] <u>0.35 mm</u>

C] 0.5 mm

D] 0.52 mm

**8-57] In the number drill series, the largest drill size is...**

A] 102 mm

B] <u>5.791 mm</u>

C] 5.613 mm

D] 5.410 mm

**9-58] In the letter drill series**, the size of the drill 'A' is equal to ...

A] 13 mm

B] 6.08 mm

C] 6.045 mm

D] <u>5.944 mm</u>

**10-59] In the letter drill series, the largest drill size is equal to...**

A] 10.33 mm

B] <u>10.490 mm</u>

C] 12.01 mm

D] 15.00 mm

INDUSTRIAL TRAINING INSTITUTE

Monthly Test-5, Marks- 20, Date:- ________________

( Every Question Carry Two Marks )

**1-66] which one of the following is the most suitable tap for lathe work?**

A] spiral tap

B] machine tap

C] hand tap

D] left hand tap

**2-67] A die is turned with a**

A] die wrench

B] diestock

C] die plate

D] die handle

**3-68] A tumbler gear unit has**

A] a single gear

B] two gears

C] three gears

D] four gears

**4-69] The cutting edge of a solid tool is made of**

A] carbon steel

B] mild steel

C] super high speed steel

D] stelite

**5-70] The tip of a cemented carbide threading tool is**

A] brazed

B] welded

C] soldered

D] clamped to the shank

**6-71] Tool will rub against the work surfaces and the cutting force increases when..**

A] The clearance angle is more

B] The clearance angel is less

C] The rake angle is more

D] The rake angle is less

**7-72] Formation of a chip while cutting is based on the...**

A] Rake angle of the tool

B] Clearance angle of the tool

C] Wedge angle of the tool

D] Clearance and wedge angle of the tool

**8-73] The suitable cutting fluid for drilling mild steel in a drilling machine is...**

A] Synthetic soluble oil

B] Neat oil

C] Distilled water

D] Soluble oil

**9-74] Centre drilling is an operation of...**

A] Drilling and countersinking

B] Drilling and counter boring

C] Marking the centre location before drilling

D] Enlarging the diameter of a hole

**10-75] Shaft ends are centre drilled for...**

A] Supporting jobs between centres

B] Lubricating the dead centre

C] Reducing the weight

D] Assisting counter boring

INDUSTRIAL TRAINING INSTITUTE

Monthly Test-6, Marks- 20, Date:- _______________

( Every Question Carry Two Marks )

**1-80] The process of enlarging the end of a hole for accommodating the socket screw head is...**

A] Reaming

B] Spot facing

C] Counter boring

D] Counter sinking

**2-81]While choosing a boring tool for boring a given diameter, select**

A] a long tool

B] a short tool

C] a long and stout tool

D] a short and stout tool

**3-82] The cutting edge of the boring tool should be set for a small hole so that it is**

A] 0.5 mm above the center

B] 0.5 mm below the center

C] 1 mm above the center

D] in the exact center

**4-83] Bored holes are to be chamfered by using**

A] a drill

B] triangular scraper

C] a cranked boring tool

D] a flat file

**5-84] The tool used for boring deep holes is a**

A] lathe mandrel

B] sleeve

C] drill

D] auger bit

**6-85] The cutting speed for rough boring is the**

A] same as rough turning

B] same as drilling

C] same as knurling

D] same as thread cutting

**7-86] The reamer is used for...**

A] Drilling holes in thin sheets

B] Drilling deep holes

C] Removing burrs

D] Enlarging and finishing holes

**8-87] The reamer teeth are unevenly spaced because...**

A] They are easy to manufacture

B] They can reduce chattering

C] They help to cut metal gradually

D] They help to remove the reamer easily

**9-88] Which among the following is not a capability of reamers?**

A] Finishing small holes

B] Finishing any machined profiles

C] Accuracy to closer limits

D] Producing high quality surface finish

**10-89] The most important quality of any cutting fluid is**

A] emulsification

B] specific heat

C] specific gravity

D] viscosity

INDUSTRIAL TRAINING INSTITUTE

Monthly Test-7, Marks- 20, Date:- _______________

( Every Question Carry Two Marks )

**1-95] The depth of cut is given by**

A] the top slide

B] the cross-slide

C] the compound slide

D] adjusting the tool

**2-96] For mounting a lathe chuck**

A] start it by hand and then turn the power on

B] mount it on by power

C] mount it by hand

D] mount it with the help of a hammer

**3-97] The morse taper provided on drills used on lathe ranges between**

A] MT1 to MT5

B] MT1 to MT4

C] MT0 to MT5

D] MT0 to MT4

**4-98] Feeding the small drill too fast into the work may result in**

A] breaking the drill

B] bending the drill

C] cutting an oval shape hole

D] increased production

**5-99] Number of flutes in a twist drills are --------**

A] 1

B] 2

C] 3

D] 4

**6-100] Which one of the following drilling machines is used for drilling holes where electricity is not available?**

A] Bench drilling machine

B] Pillar drilling machine

C] Redial drilling machine

D] Ratchet drilling machine

**7-101] Which one of the following drilling machine is used for heavy duty work?**

A] Bench drilling machine

B] Pillar drilling machine

C] Radial drilling machine

D] Electric hand drilling machine

**8-102] The suitable cutting fluid for drilling mild steel in a lathe is**

A] synthetic soluble oil

B] neat cutting oil

C] distilled water

D] soluble oil+water

**9-103] The suitable cutting fluid for precision grinding is**

A] Soluble oil

B] Synthetic soluble oil

C] Neat oil

D] Servo Cut's'

**10-104] Advantage of using cutting fluid during grinding operation is ------**

A] 5000 surface finish

B] Reduction in cutting forces

C] Reduction in hardening of the work piece

D] All of these]

INDUSTRIAL TRAINING INSTITUTE

Monthly Test-8, Marks- 20, Date:- _______________

( Every Question Carry Two Marks )

**1-110] Which is correct angle plate used with face plate**

(A] Solid Type

(B] Box Type

(C] Adjustable Type

(D] None of them

**2-111] Face plate is made from.....]**

(A] Mild Steel

(B] Cast Iron

(C] Brass

(D] Aluminium

**3-112] Which following accessories is use for odd an uneven job turning?**

(A] Three Jaw Chuck

(B] Two Jaw Chuck

(C] Driving Plate

(D] Face Plate

**4-113] An irregular shaped work piece is turned on a Lathe] Which one of the following work holding accessories is used?**

A] Two Jaw chuck

B] Three Jaw chuck

C] Driving plate

D] Face plate

**5-114]The pads of a steady rest are made of**

A] carbon steel

B] lead

C] mild steel

D] brass

**6-115] A steady rest is used**

A] to hold jobs

B] for face plate work

C] to drive the job

D] to support the job

**7-116] A follower steady is held on the**

A] lathe bed

B] lathe carriage

C] lathe spindle

D] tailstock

**8-117] When turning long work pieces, the following is used**

A sleeve

B change gear

C steady rest

D bracket]

**9-118] Knurling operation is done at the**

A] turning spindle speed

B] high spindle speed

C] 1/3 of the turning spindle speed

D] 1⁄2 of the turning spindle speed

**10-119] Knurling is the operation of**

A] shearing

B] forming

C] turning

D] pressing

INDUSTRIAL TRAINING INSTITUTE

Monthly Test-9, Marks- 20, Date:- _______________

( Every Question Carry Two Marks )

**1-125] The number of fundamental deviations in the B.I.S] system are**

A] 20

B] 22

C] 25

D] 28

**2-126] The number of grade of tolerances in the B.I.S] system are**

A] 12

B] 16

C] 18

D] 20

**3-127] The size based on which the dimensional deviations are given is called...**

A] Actual size

B] Basic size

C] Minimum limit of size

D] Maximum limit of Size

**4-128] The size of parts made by .....] for provide interchange ability properties] (A] Measurement System**

(B] Trial and Error System

(C] Limit and Tolerance System

(D] None of Them

**5-129] Your job taper is correct if it is measured**

A above the higher limit

B in between higher and lower limit

C below the lower limit]

**6-130] When tolerance given in one side of the basic dimension, it is called --------**

A].Tolerance system

B] Unilateral tolerance

C] Bilateral tolerance

D] Allowance System

**7-131] A dimension is stated as (025 H7 in a drawing] The lower limit is -----------**

A] 24.75 mm

B] 24.85 mm

C] 25.00 mm

D] 25-021 mm

**8-132] The measured Size Of the dimensions of a component as called---------**

A] Basic size

B] Nominal Size

C] Allowed size

D] Actual size

**9-133] In the drawing the dimensions of a shaft is shown 40i 0068/ 0042, which is the size of Shaft within the tolerance?**

A] 4.0.64 mm

B] 40.042 mm

C] 40.000 mm

D] 39.998 mm

**10-134] In Hole basic system ----------**

A] The size of the shaft is made constant

B] The Size of the hole is made constant

C] Only 'allowance is given on the hole

INDUSTRIAL TRAINING INSTITUTE

Monthly Test-10, Marks- 20, Date:- ________________

( Every Question Carry Two Marks )

**1-142] A Product is said to have the quality when ...........]**

A] Its shape and dimensions are within the limit

B] It is fit for use

C] It appears to be very good

D] The choice of material is right

**2-143] The maximum clearance required between hole'30 +0.021, 0.000 and shaft 30 -0.110, 0.143 is.**

A] 0.110 mm '

B]0.131 mm

C] 0.164 mm

D] 0.143 mm

**3-144] A dimension is stated as 25 .1002 mm in a drawing] What is the tolerance?**

A] +0.02 mm'

B] +0.04 mm

C] -0.02 mm

D] 25.00 mm

**4-145] A pin is fitted in a hole] The tolerance zone of the pin is entirely above that of hole] The fit obtained will be?**

A] Clearance fit

B] Transition fit

C] Interference fit

D] Running fit

**5-146] Interchange ability is normally applied for? _**

A] Repairing of parts

B] Mass production

C] Single piece production

D] All of these

**6-147] Tolerance is given to the part size to...........]**

A] Production the part within the required permissible size error

B] Increase the production

C] Decrease the Production

D] Finish the components approximately

**7-148] Which one of the following is the clearance fit under the whole basic system?**

A] 20 H7/p6'

B] 2067/211

C] ZOG/gll ]

D] 20H/g11]

**8-149] The three classes of fits as per BIS system aré ............] ~ ]**

A] Clearance fit, interference fit and transition fit

B] Medium fit, push fit and tight fit

C] Flat fit, round fit and square fit

D] 'Sliding fit ', loose fit and shrinkage fit

**9-150] Which one of the following tolerance specifications has a maximum dimensionless than 20 mm?**

A] 20 +0.2,-0.3

B] 20 320.2

C] 20 -0.2, 0.3 e

D]m 20 +500, ~03

**10-151] Difference between the maximum and minimum limit is -~-
~~~~-~~~~ '**

A] Single informant

B] Basic shaft

C] Clearance

D] Tolerance

<div align="center">INDUSTRIAL TRAINING INSTITUTE

Monthly Test-11, Marks- 20, Date:- _______________

( Every Question Carry Two Marks )</div>

**1-160] The length of turned tapers are checked with**

A vernier calliper

B micrometer

C inside callper

D dial test indicator]

**2-161] The disadvantages of taper turning using the com] pound slide
are**

A] only long tapers can be turned

B] only very large tapers can be turned

C] only manual in feed is possible

D] only short tapers can be turned due to the restrictions of the
compound slide]

**3-162] External tapers are checked with**

A] limit plug gauge

B] taper ring gauge

C ]taper plug gauge

D] thread plug gauge]

**4-163] The use of a taper turned on lathe is ----**

A] Assist to transmit drive in the assembled parts

B] Used for Assembly and disassembly of parts

C] Give self alignment in the assembled parts

**5-164] Which type of method is used in mass production of
production of producing small length of taper?**

A] Form tool

B] Compound slide

C] Tailstock offset.

D] Taper turning attachment
~~~~

**6-165] Morse standard taper is one of the internationally accepted standards taper, which is available in numbers from--------**

A]1to7

B]1 to 8

C] O to 7

D] 0 to 8

**7-166] Which taper turning method is used for cutting steep taper?**

A] Set over method

B] Taper turning attachment

C] Form tool

D] Swivelling the compound rest

**8-167] Morse taper is used in which of the following machine components -...**

A] Spindles of lathe

B] Spindles of drill machine

C] Shanks of reamers

D] All of these

**9-168] For mass production of the taper which one of the following method is used.......]**

A] Tailstock offset method

B] Taper turning attachment method

C] Form too method

D] Compound slide method

**10-169] The major diameter of the taper is 40 mm, minor diameter is 30 mm] The total length of the job is 100 mm is tapered then offset is given by -**

A] 5 mm

B] 7.5 mm

C] 12 mm

D] 9 mm

INDUSTRIAL TRAINING INSTITUTE

Monthly Test-12, Marks- 20, Date:- ________________

( Every Question Carry Two Marks )

**1-190] Which instrument iis used for marking layout?**

A] Micrometer

B] Vernier

C] Depth gauge

D] Vernier height gauge

**2-191]** While marking with a Vernier height gauge, the work piece is generally ----------

A] Supported by an angle plate

B] Supported by another work piece

C] Held by one hand

D] Held without support

**3-192]** Which of the following is not the part of a combination set?

A] Stock

B] Square head

C] Protractor head

D] Centre head

**4-193]** A BSW threading tool is to be ground with an included angle of

A] 55∘

B] 60∘

C] 47.5∘

D] 29∘

**5-194]** The nose radius of a metric 'V' thread tool is

A] 0.144 x P

B] 0.25 x P

C] 0.414 x P

D] 0.0144 x P

**6-195]** While cutting metric external threads of coarse pitches, it is advisable to swivel the compound rest to

A] 45∘

B] 30∘

C] 60∘

D.90∘

**7-196]** The depth of B.I.S] metric thread is

A] 0.6403 x P

B] 0.6 x P

C] 0.6134 x P

D] 0.5 x P

**8-197]** Threading tools are checked for accuracy for the 60∘ angle by using a

A] Thread plug gauge

B] centre gauge

C] screw pitch gauge

D] tool angle gauge

**9-198] The number of threads per inch can be checked with a**

A] tool gauge

B] metric rule by counting

C] ring gauge

D] screw pitch gauge

**10-199] When threading, the carriage is moved along the ways by**

A] a gear train on a track

B] the feed rod spline or key-way

C] the lead screw thred

D] the hand wheel